CALLS

For Anthony,
a very fine poet.
wishing you success
and joy in the
body of love.
Aadhaa Amachr
June 3, 1999

WHEN THE BODY CALLS

SELECTED WRITINGS

MARTHA CINADER

FOREWORD BY EDWIN TORRES

HARLEM RIVER PRESS
NEW YORK

Writers and Readers Publishing, Inc.
P.O. Box 461, Village Station
New York, NY 10014

Writers and Readers Limited
9 Cynthia Street
London N1 9JF
England

When The Body Calls © 1998 by Martha Cinader
Cover image: adapted from *Exposure of Luxury*, c. 1546,
by Agnolo Tori Bronzino in the collection of the
National Gallery, London
Cover photograph: Arthur Davidson

Typoraphical design by: Tenth Avenue Editions, Inc.

This book is sold subject to the condition that it shall not, by way of trade or otherwise, be lent, re-sold, hired out, or otherwise circulated without the publisher's prior consent in any form of binding or cover other than that in which it is published and without a similar condition being imposed on the subsequent purchaser.

All rights reserved. No part of this publication may be reproduced, stored in a retrieval system, or transmitted in any form or by any means, electronic, mechanical, photocopying, recording or otherwise, without prior permission of the publisher.

ISBN # 0-86316-279-7 Trade
1 2 3 4 5 6 7 8 9 0

Manufactured in the United States of America

*This book is dedicated to Grandmother Sadie
who tells me often that she loves me.*

This book is dedicated to Grandmother Sadie who tells me often that she loves me.

Poem by Crystal Clear Waters 9
Foreword by Edwin Torres 11
From Me to You 15

POETRY
When the Body Calls 35
Crazy Mary 37
Birds and Guns 40
Around the Block 43
Lost 49
Rosebud 52
Family Values 54
Sub-talk 55
Mother's Day 58
White Linen 60
Ocean Blue 65
Virgin Mother I 66
Virgin Mother II 67
Virgin Mother III 68
Virgin Mother IV 69

PROSE POETRY
Homage to Boedicea 73
Orwell and the Anarchists 77
The Fat Lady and the Cuckoo Bird 83

TWO FAIRY TALES
A City by the Sea 89
Orimar's Flying Machine 103
(or The Baker's Daughter)

FROM THE JOURNALS OF SENATOR SIN

Letter to My Daughter 109
Un-named Flower 113
Smoke 114
A Night in the Life 117
Turning the Screw 120
Virgin Mother 121
Weather Cock 123
A Day in the Life 124

I am not an object.
I am a being.
I am not a servant.
I am a master.
I will not bow down to cruelty and hatred.
I will take a punch in pride and give one in anguish.
These words are what I live by.

—Crystal Clear Waters

FOREWORD

This book is a vessel / holding liquid for thirsty desirers / looking for a beam of recognition / in the empty spiral of this universe / where detail is opinion / one moment is all it takes to answer / when the body calls. This book is just one answer in a life of calling.

The storyteller lives inside the breath of home. Whatever home is chosen, whatever breath is owned. The desirer takes the moment we're in and stretches out its every wrinkle. In the folds are new horizons, exploding the everyday, line by line—inwards, so the shards are sort of slo-mo in their entry into gravity . . . We're brought into the world of the writer. Storytelling becomes a cycle within the writing, returning us to the beginning, where the ending is: "there is so much to do / and so much I am leaving undone." This is just one aspect of Martha Cinader's life. A complex desire for simplicity, which takes time and explodes it, line by line.

I met Martha in 1992, during one of poetry's many rebirths. At the time, many people called themselves "Poets" and "Spoken Word Artists" (still do) and through all that trendiness she was always an oddity in a land of hangers-on. Like an oracle, appearing with her flute to guide her through the galaxy, Martha spun these tales from far away, from down the block. I'm not surprised her current home is the Cinasphere; a universe from the reaches of her imagination, existing on the internet. The website is her latest project, until the next one.

A tireless worker, her radio show is an outgrowth of all the reading series she has produced. A chance for her to bring together voices and viewpoints, Martha's always been interested in the process of sharing. Her CD "Living It" is a ride in itself. Whether performing with musicians in "Po'Azz Yo'Azz" or creating radio-plays, *Marvelina* and *Mission of Love*, she explores whatever medium is used for that particular communication. How to transfer the body without losing the soul. This work is the sweat that paves your road.

If you're a single mom, teaching your child at home, while attempting to define your territory as a writer AND performer in New York City . . . irony will work its way into you. Testing her faith in dreams and sin, Martha refuses to move within the given boundaries. Her energy is one created by need. A need to state individuality, to establish position against stereotype.

This poetry travels the night path unraveled, bubbling scats under the surface. Where words get to fly, in a sort of steamy urban drawl, searching for lament from the symphony of streetlights. From broken dawn we get urban liquidy, a history rife with sensuous sensory. The backbeat is the bone. The hopped-up intervention between that world and this one. The one that skips a beat at a moment's notice. Desire and heartache. Purity and loss. This is the music of Martha's world. The street-wise raconteur, who knows you know she knows it all, but still makes you wait for the ending to see how it comes out.

"He was one of the few who survived to tell the story that no one wanted told, and he knew the story because he had gone to find it by actually living it" (from "Orwell and the Anarchists").

Taking on the persona of Senator Sin lets her skirt around feminine stereotypes. Assuming the ego's altar-piece to fill her shoes, Martha inhabits the scream at the center of her body with a dignified volume. It's the poet-at-the-center-of-the-universe aspect which is at the core of any true witness. To be honest, I don't know what kind of upbringing she had, but from when I first met her, there's always been this jazz-influenced-insanity about her and her writing which has always seemed to be some kind of crazy fuel she used for inter-planetary travel. Being a fellow passenger, I've always admired the journey.

Coursing over history, she applies some of that fuel to the facts for a natural high. During her days of organizing and hosting readings, she'd take her turn after the open mic'ers had finished. I remember on several occasions being taken on a trip, as history unfolded into Cinader-story. In this book we're brought into the lives of Queen Boedicea and George Orwell, among others. Approaching the expected by applying that fairy-tale gunslinger twist—the urban spirit at home with myth—she forms a personalized re-telling of history with a nod to Lord Buckley, not so much in language-style but in the same need to pass on the telling of these "old" stories. She wants to make sure we won't forget, like an ancient sage with a handy token, this should be required reading at history class.

Time deserves her witnesses existing in body & sound. Martha chooses to witness in words & rhythm / body references / sensuality ala senses /

exploring their relation by the medium to be explored. Whether the words are heard or seen, her many relationships result in bittersweet life at its ultimate reality. Hers is a calling to witness, and, like any true storyteller, she weaves her voice around the details of her calling . . . introducing us to our own details.

"I pass the Life Cafe, / Looking just like it did / When it opened ten years ago, / Like it's been waiting / For the last fifty years / To get fixed up a little." / ... / "Spice floats out the door of the / Carribean take out / and past my nose. / I never go in that bodega. / There's all kinds of ways / to be rude when you hand someone / their change / and plenty of places to / spend my two cents"   (from "Around the Block").

Rollerbladers glide by in their appointed lanes—zooming in the city's dry heat. A haze hanging over us—like an out of work lover, looking to settle down for a night. This book makes me think of the city like this. Makes me slow down my vision so I can see. The air around each word gives each word its city to live in. A maze of stillness permeates the air with the writer's voice. We're right there with her daughter, learning what it means to be a single mother, looking for employment, jilted by another misfit, Martha soars above us in our own home.

Listen to her, go to the kitchen, look outside, see strange clouds lounging about, tell them to leave, tell them to stay, an elderly woman takes your hand, holds it tight. An imaginary noose tightens around us as we proceed. Using straightforward language, avoiding extraneous interruption, she brings us into a paranoia which paints dream-like scenarios; where we are not totally unwilling participants, helpless but happy. Martha leads us into her chambers by the hand, pausing every now and then for reflection or escape. Below subways (see "Sub-talk") or above clouds (see "Orimar's Flying Machine").

Which leads to the fairytales. In an age of too much caution, fairytales are needed. New ones with updated moralities. Where the heroine wins the battle against the landlord. We need fairy tales to remind us of who we are: humans who need love. Is body desire? Is woman body? Is a man without "wo," a cell of desire? Does time take a call when day slips away, for an afternoon tryst with destiny?

The essence of any true poet is love; a life spent questioning spirit, resolve, our own belief systems, what gives us our chance, what lets us down. The essence of any writer is questions; like questions who question the already questioned answers of forever and now, like writers who witness their universe and disappear letting us glance at our own world. The essence of any true love is life; like a body spent in search of its senses, a morality play without happy endings, a fairy tale with a modern twist. And so, the essence of Martha Cinader's work is life as lived by a woman at home with desire.

A human existing on this planet as a woman. A mother entranced by the wonder of her child. An artist at play with the world's complexity. A writer at home with love.

Edwin Torres
New York City
May 1998

FROM ME TO YOU

"Tell me"
      the elderly and slightly cross-eyed interviewer
      leans into the table

"just what is your opinion on abortion."

"Before I answer that let me just say that I believe
in radical change now."

"Are you saying that you believe in
change by any means necessary?"

"Before I answer that let me just say that I believe
that the gateway to paradise is ministered
by priestesses who are entitled to be caressed and adored."

"Are you saying that you believe
that God is a woman?"

"Before I answer that let me just say that I believe
in a woman's right to enjoy her clitoris."

    So say I
    in my thirty-fifth year
    at the turn of the second Christian millennium.
    My publisher asked me to write this.

    He said:

"Your readers will want to know who you are."

"You saved my life."

      Hillary Rodham leans close to whisper in my ear.

"That poem you wrote
about how I should divorce Bill and run for president myself
I heard it on National Public Radio and realized you were
absolutely right!
I owe everything to you!"

      Fantasy
      not reality
      but a product of my brain
      all the same.

"Tell me about yourself"

      says the incredibly interested middle-aged man
      with well-defined muscles and
      sensual eyes and lips
      leading me across the dance floor
      strings with rhythm section.

"I was born on December 13th, 1962
in New York City.
'It took a long time'
That's what my mother said."

      I knew nothing then about the clip of scissors,
      the tearing of tendons,
      swollen and forbidden breasts,
      the spilling of my mother's blood.

"Maybe someone in my family will want to sue me.
Not if I stick to the facts."

      My mother says I remember things
      that I imagined.

"The facts are.
I am a writer.
I write poetry
true stories
imagined stories
published
in magazines
and newspapers
and books
and on the World Wide Web.
I've written radio dramas
which were heard by
uncounted ears in
the United States
and Germany.
I've been translated into German
and Japanese.
I also like to interview writers.
To date I have met with Victor Cruz, Ana Castillo, Ken Kesey,
Dr. Clarissa Pinkola Estes, Kate Horsley, A. A. Carr, Lan Cao,
Nora Okja Keller, Barbara Chase Riboud, Walter Mosley,
Walter Bishop, Jr. (he wrote poetry too), Sarah Peretsky,
Dorothy Alison, Darius James, Rudolfo Anaya
and a few people
I can't think of right now.
I hope to interview
Chitra Banarjee Divakaruni
and Joan Didion
one day.

    That's a fact.

    Sometimes I earn money with this spinning of words.
    Sometimes I use a pseudonym.
    Sometimes I've coded websites for corporations with
    questionable business practices,

answered telephones for nonprofit organizations,
served cookies, in a tight T-shirt, to strangers,
sold clothes made by unknown hands,
modeled my hair and body in photos and
down runways and once on ABC television,
to earn money."

"So what are you exactly?"

asks the college radio interviewer
live on the telephone
from middle America.

"I would just like to say that
I am a storyteller.
I find stories
in the present, past
and future
and repeat stories
and make up new stories
from old stories.
I am a poet.
I recite words
strung together
like prayer beads
with bassists
and percussionists
and pianists
and horn players
and dj's
over ISDN lines
on public radio
and commercial radio
and public television
and cassettes
and vinyl

and CD's
in nightclubs
and libraries
and cafés
and schools
and theaters
and bookstores
and shelters
and parks
and gardens
and bars
and restaurants
and galleries
and demonstrations
and fund-raisers
and private parties
and big festivals
and alone."

"Are you saying that you are a multi-media artist?"

    asks my accountant.

"Were you a middle child?"

    A brunette therapist
    whose family survived the camps
    asks me from where he sits
    in a chair
    behind the couch
    I am lying on
    self-consciously.

"I'm the second of five surviving children.
The firstborn son
was run over by a car

on a night already
mangled with my mother's pain."

    More spilling of my mother's blood.

"How do you know that?"

"I can't tell you exactly how I came by
everything I know
except that I get it in bits
and pieces,
oddly shaped mosaic tiles
which form a pattern
I must hover over
to see."

"Why do you suppose you can't remember
exactly the events of your life?"

"Before I answer that I just want to say that
a few years ago
my former governess
heard me on the radio
while she happened to be driving through
New York City
and called me at the station
and we got together for tea."

    Some things would be denied.

"I get the most current information
about my family
from the newspapers,
and the World Wide Web
and my hairdresser.
Mostly I hover in dreams."

I had one last night.
I'm in a sprawling house
with my family.
I can get lost in this house.
I have been here before.
I rediscover unused rooms
as I do every time I am here.
They are sunny
and there are many windows.
I go to ask my mother if I can use the rooms.
She says:

"I don't want you to have any male prostitutes in those rooms."

Actually it is my father
and my brother
who come into my bathroom
while I am lying in the tub.
They step on the edge of the tub
with their dirty shoes.
There are men
watching me from the windows
and trying to get in.
Then I hear:

"Ladies and Gentlemen, Rahsaan Roland Kirk"

My powermac is set
to start up at six A.M.
My first lucid thought of the day:

"I was available for a little while,
but you came on so strong
it scared me.
So I cooled out for awhile
and then I got back together

with my girlfriend."

    I get that familiar angry feeling.
    Not the way I remember it
    at all.

"Volunteered slavery,
volunteered slavery."

    On December 13th, 1962
    Relay I was launched into
    an elliptical orbit.

"Many lessons in communications spacecraft design
were learned from the project."

    I walk down the stairs
    of my duplex rental.
    I pay $1,100.00 a month to live here.
    That's a fact.
    Some of my friends think that's a lot of money.
    It doesn't amount to much compared to
    the usual mortgage and maintenance payments
    which I would be paying if I had stayed home
    if I had married a man with a career
    if I had done what might have been expected of me
    if anything indeed was expected of me.

    I'm straying from the facts.

"I live in East Harlem."

"Isn't that a dangerous neighborhood?"

    I decide to change
    my dancing partner's complexion

instant ebony black
with a wry knowing expression.

"Aren't you a little pale
to be swishing around
that part of town?"

    he asks as he dips
    me back
    off my balance
    and kisses me on the lips.

"I take taxis home from the East Village
late at night.
I used to live in the East Village
in spots which were never too far from where my grandmother
my father's mother was born.
I did an alternate reality
of the American dream,
a wormhole voyage into
previously unimagined dimensions
which the geometric rules of my upbringing
could not accommodate."

"Are you saying you went from riches to rags?"

    This Sunday morning interviewer
    really wants to know me
    as a person
    a writer
    whose publisher thinks
    her readers might be interested in
    knowing something about.

    He's more attractive than I thought
    when I first laid eyes on him.

I think he must work out.

"Before I answer that I just want to say that
I used to live on Park Avenue.
I went to the Spence School for girls.
That was after I went to Kent Place
in Montclair, New Jersey and then moved to
Alburquerque when my father
purchased a large portion of
the First National Bank in Albuquerque
where I went to Manzano Day School
and then the Sandia School
and then moved to New York City
after my father left the bank
because of circumstances which
were hard for his twelve-year old daughter
to comprehend.
Finally I dropped out of my first year
at New York University
after my creative writing teacher
recommended Buddhism to me
because she thought my writing
signaled that I was in trouble
with the Universe."

    I was in trouble.
    But I don't think the Universe was troubled with me.

First I open my e-mail
then I go to the bathroom.
I hear the modem connect
know that messages are piling up
on the screen.
I wash my hands
go into the kitchen and smell the jasmine.
My favorite flower thrives

in the southern exposure.
I pour filtered water into the teapot
put the pot on the stove.
Turn the gas on.

These are all facts.
I usually have e-mail from Europe in the morning.
Another message from Brussels.

"You're asking for too much money.
We don't have it in the budget
to pay your transportation
and pay you too."

I update the poem of the day
and the story of the week
on Planet AUTHORity
and telnet into my account
to find out how many people
have looked at www.cinader.com
in the last twenty-four hours.
Holding steady at a modest 300 file transfers
per day.

"I adore instant publishing
but I don't make a living at it."

I walk back upstairs.

"Time to get up!"

No response.

"Hey Good Morning.
It's time to get up."

I hear a grunt from the bed.
The light of my life.
My pleasure,
my pain
my reason.

"Come on now, let's get going!"

"All right in a minute."

"Tell me about your religious upbringing"

    asks a voice floating
    to a point directly above
    my ripe reclining figure
    on the couch.

"At her age I had never seen
the inside of a church or temple.
I didn't miss it as far as I can remember.
I knew my father was Jewish
from the Bronx.
I knew my mother was a Calvinist Protestant
from Den Haag.
My mother's parents both died of cancer
by the way.
As far as I could tell they were upper economic class Americans.
But something made my father decide
to become a Christian,
an Episcopalian.
Maybe it was the desert air.
He was baptized and so were the rest of us
at the Church of St. John the Divine
in Albuquerque.
His conversion included the new practice
of reading the Bible after dinner in the evenings.

I joined the choir
and the hand-bell choir too
and fell in love
with a boy in the tenor section
who also played the biggest bells
in the hand-bell choir.
I read the entire Bible.
I was very devout for about a year
and a half.
Then we moved to New York City
and I converted to
art
at the age of thirteen.
What else is there
at the dawn of the 21st Century?"

"Let's stick to facts."

    says the gossip columnist/host
    to my face on a video screen.

"These are facts.
I started writing poetry
at the age of thirteen
when I was overwhelmed
with confusion
and desire
and despair.
I kept journals which
I destroyed
and wrote poetry
no one paid any attention to.
I read many novels.
I refused to go to church.

At the age of fifteen

I started studying the flute.
I took lessons.
I got a part playing solo on stage
in an off-Broadway production
of "Mulatto" by Langston Hughes,
which went on to win an Audelco award.
I had an affair with a married man
who gave me drugs
I eagerly consumed
and brought me to
the Grand Hyatt Hotel
when my parents thought
I was visiting my girlfriends.
I ran away from home for a week
and caused my parents a lot of distress.
I started seeing a therapist some time after I came back."

"So you're a rebel"

>Prince Charming whispers in my ear
>still leading me around
>in dizzy circles on the dance floor.

"I graduated from high school
when I was seventeen
with honors
and college credit
at about the time
I started hanging out in Jazz clubs
and discovered how limited
my education was.
No one had ever told me about Charlie Parker.
I turned down an opportunity to study
the classics at St. John's University.
I quit working in the customer service department
at my father's company.

My father demanded the keys to the house.
I went and got five hundred dollars cash
on my credit card
and moved in with a musician
(I traveled with him
from the East Village
to Amsterdam
across the face of Europe,
gave birth to his daughter
in Paris
returned alone with her
to a studio on Eleventh Street
when she was three
and I was twenty-six).
My father called me a thief
and changed the locks on the door.
That was the biggest favor
he ever did me
in my life."

"Are you saying that you believe you are a victim?"

      asks the gossip columnist/host,
      the Sunday morning interviewer,
      Hilary, the college radio call
      my therapist and my lover
      in unison.

"Before I answer that let me just say that
my feet belong on the ground
life is a dream
things are never what they seem
and the good things are free."

"Aren't those lyrics from a song?
Didn't I hear that on Hot 97?"

"Oh were you tuned in?
Yes it actually made it to commercial radio
ten weeks in a row
but let me just say
that I am a volunteer producer
at a non-commercial radio station
and I believe in voting with my dollar."

"Are you saying that you believe
that you, an individual consumer,
can make a difference?"

> He leans closer and looks down my blouse.
> I see that he has a bulge in his pants
> but the camera is focused on my cleavage.

"Before I answer that let me just say
that I have accepted money
to perform my services
from cigarette companies
who flew me in airplanes
which may well have been supplied
with fuel from Nigeria.
I can't be sure to be honest.
Sometimes I buy vegetables at the supermarket
even though I know
they are covered with invisible chemicals.
I've probably worn clothes which were made by slave labor.
I believe Mumia Abu-Jamal should be heard
on public radio.
I believe that AIDS in Africa
is really spelled I.M.F.
I believe in radical change now
like I said before."

"Cut. Cut. Commercial break.
The producers want to cut to tape."

>Out of time.
>Out of space.
>See you but not on television.

POETRY

WHEN THE BODY CALLS

Recorded on the CD "Living It" on Liquid Sound Lounge Recordings

In that place and time
when the pulse of generations
beats in the ears,
an internal song
of blood and guts and longing
singing in the bones,
untold sorrows
desires and
unfulfilled desires
moments of triumph
all bending toward that moment
stretched across the universe
when the body calls.

The body,
countless cells
resurrecting themselves
planets spinning around stars.

The body,
a vessel holding water from the well
virgin water from the ocean depths
running water from the mountain streams.

The body,
a ship with the wind of
whispers of the dead
in its sails
searching for a beam of light
a message of home.

The body,
manifesting itself in
every direction from the body
animating thoughts in brains
in bodies bent to new tasks.

The body of need.
The body of dreams.
The body of people
rising from ashes to struggle,
resurrected from the dead
when the body calls.

CRAZY MARY

"Mary tell me your symptoms."

"Yes Doctor"

My veins are running
with plagues of the century
injected into me when I was born
in the middle of a secret experiment.

My stomach's full
of poison grapes
pork tomatoes
meat of demented animal dreams.

My intestines are the color
of fd&c red #13
white bread
and blue babies.

My liver sweats
carbon monoxide
cigar smoke dreams
and free drink tickets.

My throat gets sore
swollen
constricted with emotion
and itches in offices.

I hear subway screeches and
screams and scurry up escalators
run from the sound of shooting bullets
and lewd comments.

My hair is turning gray
like cement
like storm clouds
like institutional turkey.

My eyes
are red, itchy, swollen
tell my story
shed many tears.

"But Mary you are HIV negative."

"Yes Doctor."

"Mary tell me about your family."

"Yes Doctor."

My son is in prison
labors for his rent
and his brother buys
canned goods at the supermarket.

My daughter gets raped every day
by a thousand pairs of eyes
and her sister sells sexual favors
to the president's club.
My grandson can't breathe
without air-conditioning
and inhalers and codeine
and he's allergic to his mother's milk.

My uncle is across the water
cutting down rain forests
and my brother
has malignant skin cancer.

My aunt's across the border
working in my father's factory
and my shirt
is stained with her blood.

"But Mary, I don't see any blood."

"Yes Doctor."

BIRDS AND GUNS

Published in A Gathering of the Tribes *issue #6, 1996*

It's four o'clock in the morning.
My Songbird across the street,
jubilant songbird
perched in the tree
over the burnt-down fun house
in the vacant fenced-in lot.
Songbird has begun the dawn song.
I am amazed.
I don't know what kind of
songbird she is,
visits me in the mornings,
messenger of Goddess
come here to nest where
artificially inseminated plots
are daily hatched.
Messenger announcing a new day.
The chirping birds join in,
Sparrows I think.
I don't know birds.

A loud explosion rocks the dawn,
arrests my songbird's song.
How far away is that?
I remember the kid on the corner
the day before,
as high as my navel,
head cleanly shaved,
gray automatic weapon in his hands,
master of the land
on which he could stand.
The cops asking
"Where does this boy live?"

Getting no answer from the kids.
Three more explosions
follow my heartbeat.
Silence rings in my ears.
I don't know guns.

I don't know guns or birds.
I remember the Vietnam War on television
with Quaker Oats and fresh O.J.,
death lists and history lessons
about heroes and God
and guns and God
and honor and guns
and god and honor and guns.
What about the birds?
I don't know guns.

I know them from visions.
I see them on cop shows and PBS Safaris.
I hear them from my window.
How far away is that?
Across the street
over a desert
in North Korea
or exploding in my head
or in my memory?
How far away is that?
Under an ocean
last year
tomorrow?

My Songbird started singing
at five in the morning
and I was amazed.
I was amazed.

AROUND THE BLOCK

My front door slams shut
behind me,
no time for a desperado
to slip in
find shelter,
steal something,
take a quick sniff
or jab.
I blink in the bright hot sun.

A neighbor
I've never noticed
stands among his possessions,
newly evicted,
selling a wok, a bed frame,
for pocket change,
can't carry it on his back
can't leave it either.
I smell an ocean breeze.

The wall woman watches
from her painted window,
cigarette hanging
between her lips,
baby in chains
in her belly,
big brown eyes
never blinking.
The birds are taking a siesta.

An old young man
shuffles by me,
back bent and bony,
talking to someone invisible

about the ways of white men,
tin cans making music on his back
like Santa's sack
in the summertime.
Weeds are growing in the sidewalk.

A man from the offices
of the United Homeless
is curbed on the curb.
Last night the evening news
showed twenty seconds
of his speech to city hall.
Right now he's in the gutter
with a bottle in a paper bag.
The leaves on the ginkgo trees are green.

The twins and their brothers
are on the corner
just like every day.
I nod to the Super
driving away in his pickup.
Kids leave the Arab grocery
with candy,
adults with cheap beer.
Dead rat smell is lingering.

The old drunk always sitting
on the pile of *Village Voice*s
invites me to suck his dick,
tells me it tastes good,
young man bumping into me
and not looking back,
bottle crashing and splintering
around my heels.
A cloud passes over my head.

The imported punks
have claimed the terrace
of the Rainbow Café,
closed for months now,
asking me for money
for beer,
heads in each others laps,
arms extended lazily.
A furry dog curls motionless in the heat.

Across Tenth Street
uniformed police
stand in neat rows.
Their command center on wheels
catches me on video
as I turn left
and pass the nursery school
for mostly white kids.
The library is closed.

The steps accommodate
a few drunken homeless men
who inform me that
I am too skinny
for their taste.
A little baby trips by
taking its first steps
hanging on to his mother's hand.
The library is closed.
The library is closed.
Too late.
I'll have to come back.
I pass the Life Café,
looking just like it did
when it opened ten years ago,
like it's been waiting

for the last fifty years
to get fixed up a little.

Earl Cross the trumpet player
used to hang out at Life
and pick up white girls.
He used to know the melody
of any song you could name,
jazz, pop, whatever.
I see a woman kick a man
in the stomach and run away.
He just walks away.

I see Fran
former fashion model
wearing a helmet
and rubber gloves,
pants hitched and belted
around an anorexic waist,
walking in the middle of the street
unchanged since the day
her daughter disappeared.

Spice floats out the door of the
Caribbean takeout
and past my nose.
I never go in that bodega.
There's all kinds of ways
to be rude when you hand someone
their change
and plenty of places to
spend my two cents.

There's a meeting going on in
the church of God Incorporated.
They're raising the roof off the Joint.

There's no windows, but
the sound of singing is busting out
of the cracks.
Across the street the neon
Jesus saves sign
lights up for the night.

There's a posse hanging out
in the one-chair barber shop,
dance music blasting from inside.
Someone's getting his head shaved
with a unique design.
A young man is washing his car
and posturing for the giggling girls
coming up the block behind me.
I get splashed with the hose.

The windmill on the roof across the street
casts a shadow
on some solar panel frames.
Someone told me a young uptown girl
was raped in the basement of that building
after plastering walls all day.
A young dark man was accused.
The solar panels never arrived.
The windmill never fully turned.

A man offers me
crack,
dope,
tells me
he can get me
whatever I want.
When I don't reply
he claims
we met before.

Then he tells me I should smile.
Then he calls me a bitch.
When I reach my door
to my little cubicle,
my evicted neighbor
and his stuff
are gone.
Just another little turn
around the block.

LOST

I took off my clothes
and found skin,
peeled off my skin
and found bone structure,
plucked out my eyes,
and saw memories,
plugged my ears,
and heard my heart beat,
flung my limbs
across the continents
and commanded them to return
to me
but they did not return.

I searched for myself
in holy places
black faces
red traces
yellow cabs
green valleys
under granite
and concrete
and comforters
and wall to wall carpets.
I sifted through shiny pebbles,
gazed into crystal clear waters,
made mud pies with hands and feet,
prayed to a nameless holy spirit
and got lost.

I searched with meditation.
I pressed every pressure point.
I learned folktales and myths.
I searched for myself among African bones

laying in the bed of the Atlantic.
I sifted through the ashes in Buchenwald and Dachau.
I chased after the whispers of witches
burned on crosses.
I danced in a Siberian wind storm.
I drifted down the Nile and
got off in a place where
no one knew
where they came from.

I got lost
looking for myself.
I got lost
in conflict and confusion and commotion.
I got lost
in a sea of liquid lies lapping languorously along my edges.
I got lost
telling lies.
I got lost
listening to lies.
I got lost
living lies that were true.
I got lost
looking for my grandmothers and my grandfathers.
I got lost
on a telephone line.
I got lost
inside a TV screen.
I got lost
on my web page.
I got lost
buying things I didn't need.
I got lost
in the arms of lovers,
in the eyes of strangers,
in the pages of rewritten history.

I got lost
in a beggar's bowl.
I got lost
on a riff.
I got lost
standing on my hands,
asking why,
following misinterpreted signs,
just waiting for the sun to shine.

I took off my clothes
and found skin,
peeled off my skin
and found bone structure,
plucked out my eyes
and saw memories,
plugged my ears
and heard my heart beat,
flung my limbs
across the continents
and commanded them
to return to me.
But they did not return.

ROSEBUD

From Marvelina, *a radio serial recorded live on WBAI Radio, NYC*

Like a tight-wrapped rosebud
shy to Jack's frosty fingers
beneath each layer of petals
falling away,
I am oblivious to all the signs
along the fast lane
as if I know secretly
some other route.

Beneath, behind,
around, beyond
the arrows
pointing down the road
to annihilation
I am poised wide open to feel
the sun upon my petals.
But they simply wither and
are trampled on.

But like a tight-wrapped rosebud
forever begging
to be explored
singing sweetly
to the bee
about my honey pots
stored in unexplored pathways,
I am anxious
to receive a visitor.

Deep within my chambers
a placid lake
reflecting the divine image

of my soul,
rippling with the rhythm eternal
is still wet.
Dewdrops individually collected
each morning
lap along the shores
in the evening,
inviting you to be anointed.

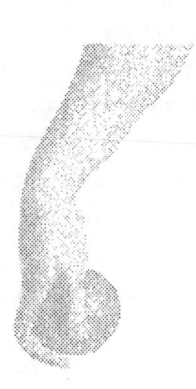

FAMILY VALUES

My husband ran away
with the baby-sitter
and they both left
their dirty dishes in the sink.

The baby-sitter's pregnant
her father disowned her
and my husband
ran away with the maid.

The maid has been crying
since she had an abortion
and my husband
ran away with his secretary.

The secretary was raped
by the chairman of the board
and my husband
ran away with the schoolteacher.

The schoolteacher got fired
and works in a whorehouse
and my husband
ran away with a very young waitress.

The maid told the waitress
that my husband's her father
and my husband
ran away to a monastery.

Now I fix rice and beans,
and the baby-sitter, the maid, the secretary, the schoolteacher,
and the very young waitress
all come to dinner.

SUB-TALK

Sub-sub submarines and jelly beans
are some of my favorite things.
Lookin' in the window what do I see?
Candy Man is comin' t'get me.
Gonna hold my mama's hand
and walk around that crazy man.
The sign says you're not 'sposed
to ask for money in the subway.
Cuz then people don't wanna ride.
And they gotta hide their money.
And their gold chains and diamonds and stuff.
And fancy watches.
I know,
cuz there's a sign about that too.
I read real good now.
I know all kindsa things about
what'll happen when I grow up.
I don't know how big I'm gonna be.
But if I'm too big
they can make me smaller.
You know what I mean.
And if they're too small
they can make 'em bigger.
So it doesn't matter.
I can look just like Uma Thurman
if I want to.
Well maybe not.
I wanna see *Pulp Fiction.*
But my mom won't let me.
Maybe I can get Daddy to take me.
It's got stuff like in those magazines.
My Mom never buys them.
But Daddy has a pile of 'em.
I know where he keeps 'em.

I don't know why anyone would wanna do that stuff.
Everyone gets AIDS, Herpes and Genital Warts.
I think you get hemorrhoids too.
My Mom said I was right.
But sometimes I think she's not listening to me.
I read all the signs.
I'm pretty sure you have to be a man
to be a hero at night.
If he buys a condom on his way home from the subway
he doesn't get to be superman
but he gets to be something.
Maybe like a VR Trooper.
He has to buy the right kind though.
But I'm not gonna be a man.
I'm gonna be a woman when I grow up.
I don't have to worry about my face.
When I need Dr. Zismore
I'll just write his number down.
Maybe it's a beeper number.
And when my husband starts beating on me
and I smoke cigarettes
I'll just pick up my telephone.
They're called NYNEX now.
And I'll call the police.
They'll come and take him away.
And I'll be crying when they do.
And my little girl will be watching it all
at the kitchen table
by the telephone.
But she'll be OK cuz if she needs therapy
I'll write down the number.
There's a place you can get therapy that's affordable.
And doctors too
for when I get pregnant again,
so I don't have to 'dopt my baby
like in *Losing Isaiah*.

I wanna see that movie too.
That's what it's about.
I think I'll choose U.S. Healthcare.
That way I'll be covered
when I have to have my breasts removed again.
That'll be after I get addicted to cocaine
and I quit again without losing my job.
They cover that too.
US Healthcare sounds American.
And I'm American I think.
That's what my teacher told me.
But my teacher's gonna get fired.
I heard it on the News.
So maybe she's wrong.
I'm gonna write that other number too.
That one about feeling safe in school.
They have real safety experts.
They pick up the phone.
They're waiting all the time just in case.
I'm not gonna tell on nobody.
I'm just gonna tell 'em I'm scareda growin' up.
Maybe they can help me.
But I don't know.
If they could do all that
the grown-ups would be on the phone all the time.
A kid like me couldn't even get near it.
Sub-sub-submarines and jelly beans.
Lookin' in the window what do I see?
Candy man is comin' t'get me.
Gonna hold my mama's hand
and walk around that crazy man.

MOTHER'S DAY

Before I was born
my mother
loved me.

Before I knew my name
I loved
my mother.

Before I knew
I didn't know
my mother knew.

Before I knew
my daughter
I loved her.

Before she spoke
my name
she needed me.

Before my mother
knew me
she knew her mother.

Before my daughter
loved my mother
my mother was born.

Before my mother
knew her mother
her mother was born.

Before my mother
I am nothing
but love waiting.

Before my mother
loved me
I did not exist.

WHITE LINEN

Recorded on the CD "Living It" on Liquid Sound Lounge Recordings

He sits in a chair.
One man sitting
in one chair.
One elderly man.
One physically fit man.
A man with
a memory
a history
a family
a fortune
opinions
points of view.

One man
sitting in one chair
across a round table
a smooth glass table
covered in white linen.

White linen like
Grandma carried
in her trunk.
White linen like
a pure young lady
a proper lady
a pretty lady
a blonde lady
a polite lady
a grateful lady.

She sits in a chair.
One woman sitting

in one chair
across a glass table
covered in white linen.
One woman
one beating heart
one womb
one mouth to speak
two hands to reach for
a white linen napkin.
Two ears to hear words
spoken by one man.

A distinguished man.
A respected man.
A married man.
An American man.
A man who makes decisions.
A man with resources.
A man who slices his steak
and drinks red wine from a crystal goblet
and shares words with important men.

Important words.
Words with weight,
words which mean
money
and lives
and the land we stand on,
words on paper,
stamped and verified words,
and whispered words
he won't share with his daughter.

A woman.
One woman
sitting in one chair
across a glass table
covered in white linen,
who hears whispers in her nightmares.

A glass table
covered in white linen,
with two plates
four silver forks
a steak knife
two butter knives
spoons
salt, pepper
a bread basket
a rare steak
vegetables, potatoes
pasta, sauce, crumbs
drips, drops
of red wine
and blood
on the white linen.

Sitting opposite
each other,
they don't touch.
They share words.
Words working in patterns.
The same words on
the same themes.
Safe words.
Words spoken
across a glass table
reflecting words
spoken across oceans

by generations
of fathers and daughters:
commanding
obeying
demonstrating
dissenting
insisting
retracting.
She reaches
for butter
to spread
on white bread
and sees bones
and spilled blood
beneath the white linen.

One woman.
One mind.
One soul.
She knows
only what is revealed to her,
and remembers her dreams.

She is a blacklisted woman,
a woman who is ignored,
a woman without a bank account,
a mother without a husband.
She knows hopeful words.
Words of pain.
Words of discovery.
Words written on the other side
of the white linen.
Words which if spoken
would end conversation,
crack the glass table with emotion,
cause the wine to overflow the crystal chalice,

shatter the glass covering a portrait
suspended in memory,
of one man
and one woman
facing each other
across a glass table
covered in white linen.

OCEAN BLUE

My mother gave birth
in her blue depths
and cradled me
next to the undulating rhythms
of her heart.

Blue ripples of love
extended everlasting
to her shores
where she deposited me under
a blue sky.

I strode boldy away
and almost forgot where
I came from
until I saw her reflection in
a blue dream.

Flowers floated by
and I was caressed
by dancing trees
who whispered secrets to me in
shades of blue.

VIRGIN MOTHER I

She didn't know
where her feelings came from
but they were there
to be reckoned with.

She always needed
to offer gifts to the shore
so she could take
what she wanted most:

a grain of sand
to sculpt below the surface
suck into her depths
and carry forever.

VIRGIN MOTHER II

Her surface
placid and beautiful
reflected the light
and the clouds racing overhead
even while
she was shifting and changing
nurturing and protecting
whatever she could claim,
rising toward the moon
until he would turn his face away,
and falling back
on herself once more.

VIRGIN MOTHER III

She hid everything,
her ridges
reefs
and curves,
the teeming life
feeding on her
sounding her caves
never leaving her,
her gems
and sunken cities
and answers to questions,
beneath her
elastic skin.

VIRGIN MOTHER IV

She was always trying
to get to the mountain,
could only get as far
as his feet.
He never moved,
but she imagined
one day
she would surround him.

PROSE POETRY

HOMAGE TO BOEDICEA

Boedicea was bad.
She couldn't be any other way,
because everyone she knew
was tough and terrible.
You wouldn't want to cross any of them
or your skull might wind up hanging around
the neck of their favorite battle horse.
But if you didn't cross her,
Boedicea was a gasser.
She'd drink you under the table
and then carry you home,
which really turned the king on.
And he turned her on too.
So they did it right
and soon there were a couple
princesses keeping the palace up
during the wee hours of the night.
They kept on digging each other and
the princesses ripened like sweet peaches.
But one day the king woke up
and he wasn't feeling so good
and the next day he was dead.
Now Boedicea was broke up a bit
but she didn't break apart.
The king had arranged for
half his loot to go to Nero
because he figured if he didn't
Nero would take it anyway.
The other half he left to
the light of his life.
So Boedicea figured she was
the ruling queen now
and she could live with that.

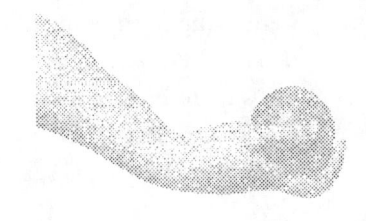

But there was a real hang-up
Boedicea didn't know anything about.
Nero wasn't feeling so agreeable
the day he read the king's will.
So he sent some slick soldiers
to take everything—
even the princesses' cherries.
And they did.
And while they were at it
they whipped Boedicea
out in the square
where everyone could get a good look
at what was going on.
Now Boedicea wasn't one to cry
or take anything lying down.
And Nero never thought
a woman would do anything
but cry and lie down.
Boedicea figured she had nothing left to lose.
The time had come to kick ass.
Especially since everyone
as far as she could walk in any direction
was as salty with Nero as she was.
So she got them all together in one place
and started rapping to them.
Everyone who knocked their ears to her speech
started remembering all the little things
and big things
the Romans had laid on them too.
Soon they were all seeing red.
Now all the Romans around
were living in the same town.
If they could have heard
the way Boedicea was carrying on,
they would have split
without packing any bags.

They never knew what hit them.
When Boedicea and her crew
were through
there was nothing left
but a few inches of superheated charcoal,
which is still there today
if you want to go looking for it.
When word got back to Nero
he sent his right-hand muscle man,
a stud named Selenius
to straighten everything out.
Selenius arrives in Brittany
a couple months later
with a couple hundred men
He gets one good look
at Boedicea and her hordes,
and all the mamas and kiddies
camped out picnicking
like war is nothing but a great big show,
and he turns around and lets them
burn down the next town
like they did the last one,
without even warning the Roman settlers
what was coming around.
Boedicea hung more skulls
around the neck of her horse.
Selenius sent word back to Nero
that he needed more men
in order to handle the situation correctly.
So Boedicea keeps carrying on,
riding her chariot,
removing Romans from the landscape
and thinking that Nero
wasn't all he'd been cracked up to be.
And he wasn't.
But his soldiers were tougher than he was.

They didn't come with their families
and they had sharper swords
than Boedicea would ever lay her hands on.
When enough of these bad boys got together
in one place
they broke up the picnic.
It didn't take them very long either.
When Boedicea saw the situation
she finished herself off
and her daughters too
before anyone else could.
Boedicea was bad.
She couldn't be any other way.

ORWELL AND THE ANARCHISTS

It was 1936. A democratic government was driving Spain around, but they didn't have control of the steering wheel. It seemed like every time they went to use the brakes or step on the gas, there was Franco telling them they had to turn right. The whole world wanted to know the story. Reporters got there any way they could so they could describe the scene to everyone else.

One of them was a young Englishman named George Orwell. Now George always wanted to go to Spain. In George's dictionary Spain and Romance meant the same thing, bright sun, beautiful women, sweet fruits, the Mediterranean Sea and, of course, Passion.

The first thing he dug on the train in Spain was that there was no first class, second class or any other kind of class. Then a scared little mouse of a man wearing four pairs of glasses warned him that he better take off his tie and put it away before he got to Barcelona. Which only made George leap off the train as soon as it pulled in, so he could go see for himself what was really going on.

Everyone and their baby sister had to wait on line for a little bread and water, but there was a wild, crazy kind of dream of freedom in the air that inspired him. The backbreaking, buckets of blood and sweat, dawn until dusk workers were the ones making the rules. Three premiers in one day hadn't known what to do about it. But they did figure out that the only way to remove Franco permanently from the highway patrol was to arm the population, so they did and they didn't regret it.

Not right away anyway. Those militiamen and women fought so fiercely, Franco had to back up and hide around the corner before he could figure out what his next maneuver was going to be. So now these same men and women were walking around wearing overalls, red and black handkerchiefs, and a straight-ahead-don't-mess-with-me kind of look in their eyes. Orwell "recognized it immediately as a state of affairs worth fighting for" and decided that instead of getting a bird's-eye view from a hotel window, he was going to go straight to wherever he was needed the most.

He went to sign up and found out right away that nothing is ever that easy in Spain. First he had to decide between the PSUC, or the CNT or the POUM or the LMNOPQXY. He asked a hundred friendly Spaniards what the difference was, but he couldn't flip the pages in his little Catalonian dictionary quick enough to keep up.

Finally he decided they were all about the same, so he joined the POUM, who happened to be Anarchists, along with a bunch of fifteen-year-olds who just wanted the bread they could smuggle home to Grandma.

George discovered that discipline among equals meant anyone could disagree with an order, but what bothered him was that they weren't learning anything about how to fire a rifle or pull a pin out of a grenade. George didn't understand at the time that the only weapons they had were themselves.

Just about the time George was convinced the POUM would have a hard time supervising a kindergarten field trip, they were ordered to the front. Speeches, bright colors, rolled blankets, red banners, the local marching band playing a revolutionary tune, and then they all piled on the slow train to Aragon with whistles, fanfare and civilization fading away as they chugged out of the station.

George got a rusty crusty past praying for German Mauser from 1896, and was seeing pictures in his brain of projectiles, skipping shards, steel, mud, lice, rats, hunger, cold and suffering. When he stepped off at the Aragon front he heard some flying bullets and ducked, but they weren't even close. The Enemy were sitting like ducks way over on the other side of a big ravine. George and his comrades didn't have anything that could shoot far enough, so they dug trenches and shouted at the Fascists over a megaphone instead.

One fighting man would yell, "Don't kill your own brothers and sisters for the man!" and a couple of those Fascist foot soldiers would get to thinking about that and slip around to the other side. Then he'd pass the megaphone along and the next man would yell, "We're having some southern-style, home brewed, spicy meatball soup tonight with some of that down-home hot buttered bread," and a few more of those Fascist foot soldiers would come on over with saliva dripping from their mouths. George was impressed and believed that he must truly be fighting on the righteous side.

For George it was simple. He joined to fight against Fascism. But Franco had been driven back by the salt of the earth, who believed they were fighting for a revolution. "Outside of Spain the papers were keeping it kind of quiet. Inside Spain everyone knew it without a doubt."

What George didn't realize right away was that the Communists didn't really want Spain to have a revolution at that very moment, on account of the fact that it would have set all of Europe to rocking and rolling so much that even those little gold pieces, and bonded papers with Communist signatures scribbled all over them, the ones sitting in those vaults over there in the beating hearts of more than one bourgeois bank, might get to jumping up and down a little too much for those very same Communists who I just mentioned previously. They wanted a little peace of mind if you know what I mean. They wanted Spain to be like it was, so the Soviet Union could be like it was.

It was very important indeed what the Soviets wanted because they were the only ones who had anything to shoot at Franco with. So the defense started training a new army in the rear and outlawed the old army fighting on the front without mentioning the fact to them at the time. Out on the front they just kept watching the same old shell named "Slow Joe" flying back and forth over the big ditch. Everyone had a cousin, uncle or great-grandma living on the other side of that ditch and had gone there every week for as long as they could remember to sell their chickens and carrots and onions and big juicy lemons. When the orders finally came for them to advance their position about a thousand yards closer it was a thousand yards closer to the beautiful priceless treasures of life who were on the other side.

George and everyone else spent seven hours in a cold marsh with smelly water and croaking frogs. Six hundred men constructed twelve hundred meters of trench and parapet without so much as one peep, snort or sneeze. Sunrise, and the bullets start flying over their heads. But they kept right on working and getting shot at. Finally they slapped together a wall of concrete with some old and cherished iron bedsteads thrown in for reinforcement.

That night, George and a few buddies crept up behind enemy lines, grabbed some rifles and got back before sunrise to the news that reinforcements had finally arrived, and after 115 days and nights he got to go on leave. George said later in his life that he "realized he had been in contact with something strange and valuable, where hope was more normal than apathy or cynicism, where comrade stood for comradeship and one had breathed the air of equality."

Even so, with lice multiplying in his trousers faster than he could massacre them, and boots with holes in the soles, he was ready for a hot bath, clean clothes and a night between clean sheets, even if he had to run the risk of appearing a little bourgeois about it. But when he returned to Barcelona, that's when the real trouble began.

This time no one went running home to pull an old trumpet out of the chest and blow a welcoming tune. The city folks just stared at him and his comrades and held their noses. The revolution had vanished. Blue overalls and militia uniforms had been replaced by smart summer suits. George suddenly realized that a whole lot of people who had worn overalls and red handkerchiefs to save their skins were happy enough to change their clothes to suit the occasion. Police were everywhere, automatic pistols strapped to their belts, while at the front the fighting men couldn't get pistols for "love or money." May 1 passed by without a single dance around a single flagpole.

On the right of the Ramblas were the Anarchists, to the left it was the Communists. It was a "war within a war within a war." The feud was going on in every paper, pamphlet, poster, and book, and was almost as big as the hang-up they all had with the Fascists. Which led George to comment later in his life that "one of the biggest mind benders of this whole disaster is to figure out that the left wing press lies just as good as the right." "It is not nice," he said, "to see a Spanish boy of fifteen carried down the line on a stretcher with a dazed white face looking out from among the blankets, and think of the sleek persons in London and Paris who are writing pamphlets to prove that this very same boy is a Fascist in disguise."

Now George never professed to exactly being an Anarchist or a Communist but he did say, "When I see an actual flesh and blood worker facing his natural enemy, the policeman, I do not have to ask myself which side I am on." So when the police stormed the telephone building and said they were taking it back, Orwell decided to camp out with the Anarchists, who had been his upright buddies all along anyway.

But the longer they stayed camped out the hungrier they got. It came down one night to one sardine each, and they didn't even have the slightest idea who was winning anyway. George had been sure he was going to spend his leave cooped up in a little hotel room with his wife, not on a roof with nothing to do but listen to his empty stomach. But then he looked out over the Mediterranean Sea and saw the British flag flying out there and a whole lot of Catalonian flags flying behind the British one and the next thing he knew the Anarchist flag came down, and his comrades had decided they were hungry enough to go home and stop fighting.

The press broke it down to everyone who had no idea what was going on. As usual, all the blame got pinned on the losers and secret police started grabbing everyone who had ever even thought for one minute that the POUM were upright and OK including wounded men, nurses, wives, great-grandpas and little kiddies. Meanwhile back on the front George felt like he was finally doing something useful and easy to understand, shooting at Fascists. Until one morning the sun rose and his luck ran out.

A loud bang, blinding light, tremendous shock, no pain, just stricken and shriveled up to nothing, knees crumpling up, falling, head hitting the ground, right arm paralyzed, thinking of his wife, wondering where he'd been hit, finding out the bullet went clean through his neck, taking it for granted that he'd said his last lines, blood dribbling out of his mouth, wondering about the man who shot him, and finally he wasn't even hung up by his own thoughts anymore.

Everything he had was stolen before he got close to a clinic, but he was alive. The doctors told him he would never do more than whisper again, declared him useless, and discharged him. George headed for Barcelona but this time his wife met him in the lobby and told him to get lost right away. An old friend walked by without even saying hello. The hotel clerk signaled him with a strange twitch of his head toward the door.

His wife wasn't dumping him. She just wanted him to stay alive. The jails were crammed with his buddies from the front, whose day in court would be a bullet in the head. George slipped into the night to find some crook or cranny to sleep. He slunk around town for days, trying to get some proper papers to cross the border.

Then George heard that his former commander had been nabbed while on an important mission to the front. George risked his own life trying to get him out. But he only succeeded in getting hot running back and forth from one official to another, none of whom could do anything about anything and all of whom looked at George himself more and more like he ought to be behind bars.

George couldn't do anything about it, but he couldn't get it out of his mind either as he and his wife chugged along on the train from Barcelona to the border. This time there was a first class and a diner's car so he invited his wife to tea for two. He was an Englishman after all. They looked so respectable at that moment, as they toasted each other's health, that the police who came through didn't bother to inspect their passports. Which was lucky for George. He was one of the few who survived to tell the story that no one wanted told, and he knew the story because he had gone to find it by actually living it. He wrote and rewrote the story and still Spain never left his dreams. He dreamt of passion and purity and the pursuit of liberty and equality. He created dreamscapes of Animal Farms and the future, all the way to 1984 and beyond.

THE FAT LADY AND
THE CUCKOO BIRD

For Dolphy Hazel (the artist)

There once was a happy cuckoo bird
going cuckoo in crazy Cuckoo Land,
until a cuckoo catcher heard
and caught him with his hands.
He carried the cuckoo in a cage,
brought him to New York City,
and sold him to Miss Ann Page
who thought the cuckoo was very pretty.
She also had a cat with claws
who knocked the cage with its paws.
One day the cage fell down
the gate flew open
the cat bound
for the ledge but the window was open.
That cuckoo flew all over New York City
looking for a pretty nest.
He flew north, south, east and west.
But nothing looked like crazy Cuckoo Land
until he came to St. Mark's Place
and saw the Fat Lady's face.
She was standing there with folded hands.

She had big breasts
a huge belly
humongous thighs
and her hair
was hanging in her eyes.
She stood inside a picket fence
and made no movements.
There was a little birdhouse hanging nearby.
The cuckoo didn't stop to ask why.

He moved right in singing a happy song
and watched the Fat Lady, but she didn't talk.
She didn't walk,
even though he waited long.
The cuckoo closed its eyes.
The sky turned black
In the window behind the Fat Lady's back
the lights went out.
No people were about
when three young men
came stumbling drunkenly
down the block on their way home to bed
and suddenly got strange ideas in their heads.
They called her fat and ugly and laughed,
pushed and shoved until she crashed,
and ran away.
The cuckoo stayed
by the Fat Lady's side
and sang until sunrise,
when the artist rose from his bed
and saw the Fat Lady had a broken head.

He didn't ask who smashed her or why.
He didn't cry.
He picked her up
and drank his cup
of coffee and fetched his pail
and wailed
the same big breasts
the same huge belly
the same humongous thighs
and her hair
was hanging in her eyes.
Many people passed by the Fat Lady every day.
Everyone looked at her in different ways.

Children couldn't wait
to run inside the gate
and hug her thighs,
looking up at her with wide eyes.
The artists and professors told
their friends that she was very old.
Tourists and fat women took photographs.
Young men pointed and poked and laughed.
Graffiti artists sprayed her while people were in bed.
Some people looked and turned their heads.
But her admirers threw money at her feet,
and actually life was pretty sweet
for the Fat Lady and the cuckoo bird.
All up and down the block his song was heard.
But a few blocks away was a hospital for the mentally ill
where a certain Sister Mary had just been given a pill
and sent away
on the coldest day.
She'd been told there was no way she could stay
the city could no longer pay.
Alone and afraid, she turned down the block
where the Fat Lady was standing like a rock.

Sister Mary fell to her knees.
"Oh please
Let me return to your warm embrace.
I don't understand this place.
When I die I don't want to leave.
It's for Mother Earth I grieve.
I'm not crazy but I'm not free.
If it was up to me
I wouldn't need money for anything
and all day long I would sing."

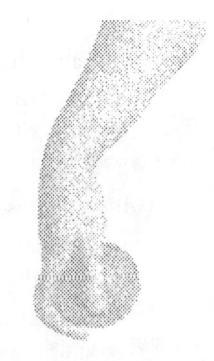

Sister Mary took the money
laying at the Fat Lady's feet
and went to buy something to eat.
One day the artist found a letter on his door
saying he couldn't live there anymore.
He had to leave the Fat Lady behind
until he could find
a new place.
He kissed her face.
The cuckoo promised to remain
But he couldn't stop the ball and crane.
The Fat Lady was broken into a thousand pieces and swept away.
After that the cuckoo bird didn't want to stay.
He flew off in search of Cuckoo Land
dreaming of the clean warm seas and the sands.

The artist did come back one day,
but it was too late to take the Fat Lady away.

He didn't ask who smashed her or why.
He didn't cry.
He fetched his pail
and he wailed
the same big breasts
the same huge belly
the same humongous thighs
and her hair was still hanging in her eyes.

TWO FAIRY TALES

A CITY BY THE SEA

There was once a coral city near a warm blue sea. The people who lived there had lovingly built, rebuilt and added on to their city for as long as they could remember. They harvested the sea for vegetables which they ate and wove into clothes. They knew how to talk to the creatures of the water, who told them about places they had never seen. The people called their city Mara, but they couldn't remember why. There was a time when the city had been so prosperous that the poorest among them were also the richest.

The Marans' inland neighbors were prosperous, but they were not satisfied. The merchants and bankers and restaurant owners living inland liked to visit the beaches of Mara in the summertime, and admired their beautiful houses with rooftops made of pearls. They talked among themselves about how they would like to live in those houses and gather up the riches of the sea to make their fortunes. One day they all got together and went to their king to tell him that he must conquer the city of Mara.

The king told his subjects that they were already the wealthiest city on the planet and really didn't need to conquer Mara, but the richest banker told the king that if he didn't lead his soldiers into battle, he wouldn't count the king's money anymore. The richest merchant told the king that if he didn't lead his soldiers into battle, he wouldn't pay the king's taxes anymore. The king's restaurateur told him that if he didn't lead his soldiers into battle, he wouldn't prepare the king's favorite dishes for dinner anymore. So the king commanded his soldiers to attack Mara.

Alas, the citizens of Mara loved peace so well they didn't even resist the king's forces. The battle was won without a fight. Within a few years the people of Mara were all poor. They worked as servants in their own homes for their neighbors, who strolled along the seashore all day and demanded the fruit of the Marans' labors every evening. These visitors didn't like sea vegetables and preferred eating fish. As the years passed the day came when the people of Mara cooked fish for their masters and forgot that they once knew how to speak to the fish, and had navigated the sea with dolphins.

If you watched the people in the streets coming and going, you could easily distinguish who were the original people of Mara, because they all had hair like silky sea vegetables. Some of the younger ones grumbled about their plight, but the elders recommended patience and forbearance. There was one young man, though, who was tired of waiting. He couldn't remember what life in Mara used to be like, because all these events had happened generations before he was born, but still he desired change.

His name was Mark. The people of Mara laughed at Mark because he always looked so serious. Every full moon they got together on the beach and celebrated with singing and dancing and feasting. The people of Mara were all accomplished musicians and dancers. They often played for their masters at weddings and barbecues but, to really appreciate their mastery, you had to hear them playing for their own enjoyment. The young men and women danced with such energy that the moon seemed to swell a little in response, but Mark would sit sullenly watching and refuse to join in the festivities.

On one such evening a beautiful young lady approached Mark with a sweet smile and invited him to dance with her. Mark gazed at her with furrowed eyebrows and replied, "How can you smile and be happy when you know that you are poor and without dignity and shall remain so for the rest of your life?" "Speak for yourself," she replied. "I may be poor but I am not without dignity." "But why should you be satisfied to remain poor while your master grows rich from your labor?" Mark replied angrily. "That's just the way it is," she said. "There is nothing that can be done about it." "Well I intend to do something about it, and I intend to do it now." Knowing that Mark always talked like this she just laughed at him and went to find herself another dancing partner.

Mark, however, had resolved that the time had come for action. He knew of a particular palace guard who always fell asleep on his watch. While Mark's family and friends danced and sang and ate and drank he slipped away to find the guard and steal his weapon. Sure enough, Mark found him snoring at his post and simply took his rifle, which was leaning against the wall. He crept through the empty kitchen and up to the king's bedchamber. Mark thought that if he could hold the king hostage, he could perhaps reason with him. The foreign king was so unused to resistance that his security had grown quite lax, and Mark had little trouble getting into his bedchamber. He stood there at the foot of the king's bed with the rifle pointing directly at the king.

The king was snoring quite loudly and appeared to be in the midst of an enjoyable dream. Mark waited for him to wake up, but even his strong arms, so used to hauling big fish from the sea, grew tired from holding the rifle at the same angle for such a long time. Finally he decided to wake the king. He moved to the side of the bed and poked the king with his newly acquired rifle. Just at the moment when the king awoke with a start, the guard, who had woken up and found his rifle missing, came bursting into the room. The king and the guard tackled Mark to the ground and threw him into prison before Mark even fully realized what had happened.

When the people of Mara learned what had occurred they were sad and shook their heads. A few of the older ones remarked to the youngsters that no good ever came from violence and it was better to have patience. Mark's mother came to visit him in jail, where he sat day after day with a sullen expression. She knew he was trying to help his people, but she didn't know how to help her son. So she brought him baked pies and sweets, which she urged him to eat. He ate them to please her but was relieved when she left and he could be alone with his thoughts once more. The jail happened to be on the beach. When the full moon rose again he watched the celebrations from the little grate in his cell by standing on his tiptoes.

The people of Mara didn't know why they assembled on the full moon, but they knew that they always had and they always would. Their masters scoffed at their celebrations, but allowed them to assemble because they didn't see it as a threat to security. As Mark watched he regretted for a moment that he hadn't accepted the young woman's invitation to dance when he had the chance. But his regret turned to bitterness. He asked himself again, "How can they all dance and celebrate like children while our mothers are disrespected and our masters grow rich off of what is rightfully ours?" He had no answer. He sighed and turned away from watching the festivities. Lying down on the bare floor, which was all he had for a bed, he closed his eyes and fell asleep while the music continued deep into the night.

Mark had a dream. In his dream he was standing alone on the beach in a storm. The waves were rising as high as the tallest building in Mara and crashing down around his feet. He was afraid but also exhilarated. Suddenly a giant fish appeared in the water. It was a beautiful silver fish with blue-tipped scales. The fish looked directly at Mark and then, to his amazement, started speaking to him in a soft voice. But the fish spoke in a language Mark couldn't understand. Mark awoke with a start. For a moment he thought he heard the voice of the fish in his little cell, but it soon faded and he realized that he was still alone. He got up and looked out the grate. There was indeed a storm, and the festivities had ended an hour or so earlier, but he didn't see a giant fish.

The next time his mother came to visit, Mark told her about the big fish in his dream. He thought she might laugh at him but she listened carefully. When he was finished she told him that her grandmother had once told her a story about just such a silver fish with blue-tipped scales. Her grandmother had said that it was the queen of the ocean. After one hundred years the fish gave birth to a daughter and then died. The daughter looked human and could walk both on water and on land, until she grew up and assumed her true form. She then became the new queen and would swim into the sea never to be seen on land again. Mark's mother told him that she always thought that her grandmother made up her stories to amuse the children. After hearing Mark relate his dream, she was beginning to think that there was more to it than that.

"What else did she tell you Mother?" Mark asked earnestly. "Well, the daughter of the Queen Fish taught the people of Coral City how to speak to the fish of the sea. The fish showed the people where to harvest their sea vegetables, where to find pearls and sunken treasures, and brought news from faraway lands. She said that was why the people of Coral City had everything they needed." "I wish I could have understood what she said to me," said Mark. Mark's mother offered him cake, which he ate, and she left.

Mark lay down hoping to have another dream of the Queen Fish, but he couldn't sleep. Finally he got up and peered through the grate at the waning moon. He started to pace back and forth in his cell. He picked up a piece of flint lying on the little ledge of the grate and started scraping a design into the stone wall of the cell. When the jailer brought him some sour milk for breakfast he found Mark putting the finishing touches on the tail of a giant fish with an open mouth.

"What are you doing?" demanded the jailer. "That will have to be removed immediately. As a punishment you will no longer be allowed any visitors." The jailer sent an old man with long hair like sea vegetables inextricably intertwined, to remove the picture from the wall. The jailer did not know that the old man was Mark's grandfather. Neither did Mark or his grandfather. Mark's grandfather had just returned to town that very morning after a fifty-year journey. He was passing by the jail when the jailer grabbed him. He was the first person the jailer saw who looked like he could be hired for a leftover meal. "You," he had said, "make yourself useful and I will give you a free lunch fit for a king." So it was that Mark, having never seen his grandfather, did not recognize him, and the grandfather, not even knowing he had a grandson, had no reason to suppose that Mark would be his.

"That's the Queen Fish," said the old man to the young man, and winked. Then he returned to the jailer and said, "That picture is carved into the wall. How am I supposed to remove it without removing the wall?" "Cover it with white paint," said the jailer. "If you will supply me with a paint and brush I will paint the wall," replied the old man. "It's in the storeroom," said the jailer. "Go get it yourself." While the jailer waited for the old man to return he looked into the open mouth of the giant fish. For a moment he thought he saw the fish flick its tongue and was relieved when the old man returned with the white paint. Mark's grandfather painted white over the Queen Fish, which only made the lines of the drawing stand out more sharply. When the jailer saw the fish even more clearly than before, he was angry and sent the old man away without giving him anything for his trouble.

That night Mark smiled for the first time in many months. He saw, in the light of the moon, that the paint looked more silvery than white. Now all he needed to do was add blue tips to the scales. For a few weeks Mark did nothing but gaze at his handiwork, and wish it would speak to him.

The time came once again for the full moon celebrations. The Marans gathered on the beach. Mark watched them, this time with admiration instead of anger. Look at how beautiful the movements of the women, how well timed with the steps of the men! Listen to the wild rhythms of the music that stirred his heart and soul! He watched them that night until the last one of them headed lazily to bed. Still he stood on his toes at the grate and gazed at the sea.

He was amazed when the waves suddenly started to rise and a storm brewed just as in his dream. The Queen Fish appeared at the crest of a giant wave and opened her mouth. Out stepped a tiny and beautiful young girl, and just as suddenly the storm subsided. It appeared to Mark that she walked down the slope of the wave and on to the shore just as the Queen Fish disappeared from view. He was even more amazed when she came directly to his grate, wriggled between the bars and stood giggling at his feet. She stood about as high as his knees.

"Why are you laughing?" asked Mark, not knowing what else to say. She giggled again, handed him a blue stone and pointed at the Queen Fish he had carved on the wall. Mark opened his hand and saw that the stone had stained his hand blue. He quickly painted the tips of the Queen Fish's scales. Then she said something to him in a language he couldn't understand, climbed back out the grate, and disappeared. Mark immediately began to wonder if she was real or if he had imagined her and soon fell asleep in a daze.

When the jailer came with Mark's sour milk in the morning and saw the blue painted tips on the Queen Fish he was very angry. He said to Mark, "That blue will have to be removed at once! As a punishment you will not be fed!" With that, the jailer dumped the sour milk on the floor and slammed the cell door as he left. He went immediately out into the street and saw an old man sitting on the beach gazing at the sea. "You," he said, not recognizing the hair like sea vegetables inextricably intertwined. "Make yourself useful and I shall give you a lunch fit for a king." Mark's grandfather stood up, walked into the jail and entered Mark's cell for a second time. "Remove that blue paint from the wall at once!" demanded the jailer.

Mark's grandfather stepped up to the wall and examined the blue tips of the Queen Fish's scales. He winked at Mark. Then the old man said to the jailer, "If you will provide me with a bucket of water and a rag, I will wash the paint off the wall." "You'll find what you need in the supply room," said the jailer. "Go and get it for yourself." Mark's grandfather left to fetch a bucket and a pail.

"You must learn to respect private property," the jailer said to Mark angrily. While the jailer stood at the entrance to the cell it seemed to him that the fish was looking at him with menacing eyes. Then suddenly, he thought he saw the fish's tail move! He closed his eyes and leaned against the wall. The old man returned with a bucket of water and started rubbing the fish scales with a wet rag. When the jailer dared to open his eyes he saw that the old man was scrubbing in circles, spreading the blue ink in a pattern that looked like ocean waves. The tips of the fish scales remained as bright and blue as ever.

The jailer had the sensation that he was being carried along a current toward the fish. "Stop that!" he yelled at the old man. "You're making it worse!" Mark laughed and the jailer stormed angrily out of his cell, turned the key in the lock, and left Mark alone once more. The jailer grabbed the old man by his shirt collar and threw him back into the street. He had been intending to give the old man Mark's lunch, which was leftovers donated by the local pub. Instead he gave it to the hungry dogs.

Mark's mother was worried. She had tried to visit him but was turned away by the jailer. She asked the jailer to give Mark the food she had specially prepared, but saw him feed it to the dogs instead. That night she sat on the beach and looked across the water as if she could find a solution to her problem written in the horizon. An old man with long hair like sea vegetables inextricably intertwined was walking on the beach. Seeing her sitting there with salt tears overwhelming her eyes he asked her why she was in distress. "My son is in jail and is allowed no visitors. The jailer has told me that he has not behaved and will not be fed. He only wanted what was fair, my poor foolish boy, but without food he will surely die."

"I saw your son just this morning, madam, and he is fine. He has created the Queen Fish on his wall for company and for this the jailer is punishing him." "What do you know about the Queen Fish?" she asked. "My mother told me about the Queen Fish many times in my youth." "And who was your mother?" "My mother lived on the beach not far from this spot. She went by the name of Marisa," replied the old man. "But that is the very same name of my grandmother who also told me about the Queen Fish, and who also lived on the beach not far from this spot!" "Then you must be the child who was growing yet in the womb when I met with great misfortune at sea." "You are my father? But my mother told me many times that you were drowned. She died of a broken heart. How can you now appear when I have exceeded my fiftieth year?" "I am truly blessed to gaze upon the face of my very own daughter before I die," replied the old man. "Indeed I see a glimmer of your mother's spirit in your eyes. She was a wondrous sweet woman."

Mark's mother and his grandfather sat on the beach until late into the night. He related to her how he had been at sea, catching fish for his master, when a great shark attacked the boat and knocked him into the water. To his utter amazement, the shark did not attack him, but instead hooked him with its fin and dragged him through the sea farther and farther from the shore. The shoreline finally disappeared completely and he despaired of ever returning with his life. After the sun rose and set over the sea three times, he was desperately hungry and cold but still alive. The shark finally arrived at the shore of a tiny island, deposited him there, and swam away.

There were no people on the island. He was desperate for something to eat. Not knowing what else to do he snatched up the piece of seaweed which had twisted itself around his leg while he was in the water. He found that it tasted good to him and satisfied his hunger. He waded into the water and discovered the same weed growing all around the island. In this way he was able to sustain himself as the years passed. He often wondered why the shark had brought him there as he gazed into the water and watched the little fish come and go. He found that without his master to order him about he had no desire himself to catch the fish or eat them. Sometimes he imagined that he could hear them talking to each other. He remembered his mother's story about the Queen Fish, who had taught the people of Mara how to speak to the creatures of the sea.

"But how long did you stay there and how did you get back?" asked his daughter. "Indeed I do not know how many years passed. I didn't keep track of the time. One day a ship came to the island and stopped there a few days to repair its sails. I begged the captain to bring me back to my family, but he declared that they were going in the opposite direction and could not make a detour. He offered to bring me along as far as the next port and I gladly accepted his offer. My daughter, that was many years ago, and I have done the best I could, without money or property or education, to find my way back home. I have had strange and wondrous adventures and been enriched with knowledge of human nature if not worldly goods, but that is a tale too long to tell while my own grandson languishes in jail and the people of Mara are still servants in their own homes."

"But what will we do?" asked Mark's mother. "They have all the advantages over us." "The people of Mara must stop catching fish on hooks," said the old man. "But they will punish us all!" gasped Mark's mother. "They must say that the fish are not biting." She brought her father home with her and prepared a bed for him.

Mark was still sitting up in his cell, gazing at the Queen Fish on his wall. He was hungry and couldn't sleep. He wasn't sure if he had really seen the little girl who had visited him, but the blue tips on the Queen Fish's scales assured him that he had. He closed his eyes for a moment, and thought he might be able to sleep for a few minutes, even with his stomach grumbling, when he heard a giggle at the gate to his cell. There was the same girl, but she had grown! He went to greet her and saw that she now stood as tall as he! He asked her again why she was laughing. She smiled and held out the key to the cell to him. He took it, and she ran away giggling. Mark quickly opened the lock to the cell, tossing the key in the snoring jailer's lap as he passed, and ran out to the beach. He saw some delicate footprints leading straight to the water's edge, but he didn't see the young woman anywhere. There was some seaweed on the sand by her footprints. Mark was so hungry he scooped it up and ate it. Nothing had ever tasted so good to him in his life.

He was free now. He thought maybe he should hide, but it wasn't daylight yet. The jailer was still sleeping. In his pocket Mark had the blue stone that the mysterious girl had given him. He walked into the streets of Mara. Before the light of dawn he painted a hundred different kinds of fish, with wide open mouths, on the walls of the city. The last one was a giant whale shark painted on the palace gate. Tired and happy with his work, Mark crawled under the steps to the gate and fell soundly asleep. He didn't notice any of the noise or confusion that was created by his handiwork when everyone else woke up and saw what he had done.

The Marans, who were always the first to rise and head to their little fishing boats on the beach, saw the fish and thought they were beautiful, recognizing all the different species Mark had painted so lovingly. When they all assembled on the beach, Mark's mother and grandfather were waiting for them. Mark's mother stood on a big rock and called out to them all. "You all know my son languishes in jail," she cried out. "Perhaps you think he is foolish and deserves to be punished. But I ask you, does my son deserve to die of starvation and loneliness?" The Marans shook their heads in agreement that he did not deserve to die. The young woman who Mark had refused to dance with called out, asking, "What can we do? They have weapons and we have only ourselves."

Mark's grandfather stepped forward. The Marans, who respected their elders, became quiet in the presence of the old man with hair like seaweed inextricably intertwined. "You must go out as if you are going to catch the fish, but come back at the end of the day and say that no fish bit any of your hooks." At this suggestion they all started talking among themselves. Without raising his voice the old man continued. "You can spend the day harvesting seaweed instead. You will find that if you eat it you will not go hungry." The Marans agreed that they would do this, climbed into their boats, and headed out to sea.

When their masters awoke they also saw Mark's fish paintings. They were angry and asked who had painted on their walls without permission. The big open mouths looked scary. Some people even imagined that they saw the fish moving. They called the old women of Mara and demanded that they wash the paintings off the houses and walls immediately. The old women went to fetch buckets of water and rags and tried to wash the paintings away but, just like before, instead of washing away the blue swirled around the fish and looked like the sea. The foreigners became angry and frightened when they saw that the fish could not be removed and went to complain to the king.

The jailer, not intending to feed Mark any breakfast, was the last person in Mara to wake up that morning. He was having a dream about a giant fish with snapping jaws chasing him across the beach and woke up just as the fish was catching up to him. He was sweating and looked about wildly as if the fish might still be chasing after him. "It's the boy's fault. This is all the boy's fault. I will make him pay for giving me bad dreams," the jailer declared. He picked up his keys from his lap and went to the cell, intending to whip Mark to make himself feel better. When he discovered that Mark had escaped he hurried to the castle to tell the king.

Along the way he saw the fish painted on the walls, each one bigger than the one before. It seemed to him that they were going to leap off the walls and chase him with snapping jaws. He started to run and did not stop until he got to the palace gate.

The jailer found a crowd already assembled at the palace gate, gaping at the painting of the whale shark. The king looked out his window, as he was accustomed to do in the mornings for a little while before he did anything else. He saw the crowd but couldn't see what they were pointing at. He assumed they were pointing at him. Thinking he'd forgotten an important civic duty, he put on his robe over his pajamas and his crown on his head and commanded his soldiers to let down the gate.

Imagine his surprise when the gate came down and all his subjects came running through, practically knocking him over in their rush to get inside. The king's crown fell into a puddle, but he still had a kingly voice. "Silence!" he commanded. "I will speak to all of you one at a time!" He told his soldiers to give out numbers and commanded everyone to get in a line according to their number. The bankers and merchants and restaurant owners all jostled to get the first numbers. It just so happened that the jailer got number nine hundred ninety-nine.

All that day the king sat locked inside his castle listening to story after story about fish paintings on the walls of Mara. He asked each person if they knew who had painted the fish. Each banker, each merchant, each restaurateur replied that he had no idea. It wasn't until the king got to number nine hundred ninety-nine, and the jailer told him his story, that the king thought of Mark. He had forgotten all about Mark after he had sent him off to jail.

The king immediately ordered his soldiers to find Mark. He commanded once again that the gate be let down. Just as the gate touched the ground an old woman wearing a shawl appeared at the top of the hill and approached the king. She spoke to the king in a language he couldn't understand. "What gibberish is this?" asked the king. The old woman laughed. "You dare to laugh at the king? Stop laughing!" he commanded. The old woman laughed even harder, holding her sides and giggling so hard she fell to the ground. "Seize that disrespectful woman and throw her in jail!" commanded the king.

A few soldiers closed in on the old woman, but at the last moment she leapt up like an agile nymph and was gone over the top of the hill before the soldiers could focus on her and aim their rifles. The soldiers and the bankers and the merchants and the restaurateurs and the king followed the chase all the way to the beach, where they found delicate footprints leading right to the water's edge. The Marans were just then returning to the shore with boats full of seaweed, and found themselves standing face to face with their foreign masters.

"Where is our fish?" demanded the merchants and the bankers and the restaurant owners. The Marans all shrugged and each replied, "The fish didn't bite today." "They're all liars," yelled the jailer. "What will we eat for dinner tonight?" wailed the richest banker. The king's subjects turned around and looked to the king for an answer. The king pointed at his soldiers. "Take some of those boats," he commanded, "and go out and see if you can catch some fish." The soldiers dumped the seaweed onto the beach and rowed a few of the Marans' boats out into the sea. They cast the fishing lines and waited, but not a single fish bit a single hook for over an hour.

"It's a trick!" said the jailer. "Then you go catch a fish," said the king. "But sire," said the jailer, "I don't know how to catch a fish. Isn't there someone better qualified for the job? If something happened to me who would carry the keys to the prison cells?" The king pointed at the banker. "Then you go," the king said. "But sire," said the banker, "I only know how to eat fish. Isn't there someone better qualified for the job? If something happened to me who would count your money?" The king pointed at a merchant. "Well then you go and catch a fish," he said. "But sire," replied the merchant, "I only know how to sell fish. Isn't there someone better qualified for the job? If something happened to me who would there be to pay your taxes?"

Everyone was looking at the king. "You are our hero!" yelled his subjects. "We know you can catch a fish!" The king reached up to straighten his crown and realized that he had left it lying in a puddle back at the castle. He strode boldly to a fishing boat, removed his robe and handed it to an old man with hair like sea vegetables inextricably intertwined. As the king stepped into the boat, everyone laughed because he was still in his pajamas. Realizing how ridiculous he looked, the king was determined to catch an extra big fish.

He rowed the little boat out into the sea. Suddenly the wind started to blow and the waves became higher. The soldiers' boats started tipping, and they headed back to shore. The king was determined now to prove he was a hero, so he rowed out a little further. Suddenly his boat rose up on the crest of a swelling wave and he saw the gaping jaws of a giant whale shark rise up from the wave, and he was swallowed whole along with the boat. He's still rowing around in there today eating plankton and looking for a way out.

When the king's soldiers saw the king get swallowed up they shot all their ammunition out to sea, but the whale shark had already returned to the ocean depths. The king's subjects were astonished and frightened and started running back to the city for the safety of the castle. The Marans gathered up the seaweed and carried it back to the city in their baskets.

Meanwhile, Mark had finally woken up feeling refreshed. Not hearing any sound at all, he crept out from under the gate. Seeing it open, and the castle courtyard empty, he went inside and immediately painted a giant blue fish on the courtyard wall. He saw the king's crown lying in a puddle of water and wondered what had happened to the king. He picked the crown up and wiped it off. Just then, he saw the king's subjects running toward the castle with his soldiers following behind. Mark quickly closed the gate. "Shoot!" yelled the king's subjects. The soldiers shot their rifles but were out of ammunition. Realizing they were locked out of the castle and had no weapons, the foreigners ran all the way back to their own city, where they and their offspring have stayed to this day.

When the Marans trudged into the coral city carrying their heavy loads of seaweed and saw Mark smiling at the castle gate, they placed the crown on his head and went happily to their homes. Mark and his mother and his grandfather sat together for the first time and shared a meal. The old man told stories about his adventures deep into the night.

On the next full moon the Marans had a celebration like never before. Mark danced with every young woman in the city. When it was over and he went to sleep, he had a dream in which a young girl showed him how to make clothes with seaweed. On the next full moon he asked the same young woman who had asked him to dance many moons before if she would be his wife. That night, he dreamed of a young woman showing him how to make paper with seaweed. On the third moon of his reign as king, Mark was married. On his wedding night he dreamt that an old woman dove with him into the sea, who introduced him to the sea creatures. The citizens of the deep spoke to him and showed him where there were pearls and other buried treasures.

Mark shared his dreams with the people of Mara, and they never again lacked for anything that they truly needed.

ORIMAR'S FLYING MACHINE
(OR THE BAKER'S DAUGHTER)

Based on an idea by Jay Rodriguez

Once upon a time there was a kingdom which was always cloudy.
It was so cloudy that people got lost and were late for appointments.
The kingdom was on top of a mountain between a lake and a forest.
The lake stretched as far as anyone could see in any direction.
The forest was so thick no one had ever found the edge of it.
Or at least no one ever returned to speak of it.

Prince Orimar was born looking for the sky.
When he lay on his back he pointed at the clouds.
When he sat up he threw pebbles at the clouds.
When he started walking he flew kites in the clouds.
When he started talking he asked what was beyond the clouds.
He used his hands to make mechanical wings and other machines.

Orimar was always testing his machines.
Mostly, when he jumped off the mountain, he fell in the lake.
But one day he actually stayed in the air and flew away.
No one saw him go.
They had all stopped watching his dives a long time ago.
Prince Orimar got blown around but he kept flying higher.

A flock of ducks emerged in front of him.
He followed the ducks south.
Orimar wanted to see the sun.
He also wanted to ask the sun a question.
He wanted to know why the sun never shone on his kingdom.
But Orimar didn't know how long his own fuel would last.

It started getting warmer and Orimar started sweating.
Then suddenly the sheltering clouds disappeared.
Orimar blinked in the brightness but kept his eyes open.
The sun was more dazzling than he had ever imagined.

Orimar was so overpowered he was afraid to speak.
But the sun noticed the unusual-looking bird right away.

"What kind of bird are you?" asked the sun.
"Are you talking to me?" asked Orimar.
"You answered me," said the sun.
"I'm not a bird but a prince," said Orimar.
"I am the first person in my kingdom to see your face.
Could I persuade you to pay us a visit?"

Suddenly there was a thunderbolt and the clouds started to rain.
"I think I know where you're from," said the sun.
"When I think of it I am so sad I don't want to shine anymore."
"You don't want to shine on my kingdom?" asked Orimar.
"When I think of it I don't want to shine at all," said the sun.
There was another great thunderclap and the clouds started to hail.

Orimar thought the clouds were closing in on him.
"It seems to me that you must keep shining," said Orimar.
"What could make you so sad that you don't want to shine?"
The sun paled and spoke in a quavering voice.
"There was a time when I visited your kingdom every day.
There was a young girl there who rose every morning to greet me.

"She was the baker's daughter.
She took my golden glow and put it in the muffins she sold.
Everyone who ate them was happy and filled with love.
One day the prince came into the shop himself to buy a muffin.
When he saw my golden glow shining in her face he fell in love.
She was honored and gave her heart to him freely."

"Why should that make you sad?" asked Orimar.
He was worried he was going to crash into the water soon.
"Because the king told the prince he should marry a princess.

After that the prince only saw her apron and not her warm smile.
Soon he married a forest princess and forgot the baker's daughter.
But she never forgot him."

There was another thunderclap and the clouds started to sleet.
Orimar was buffeted around by a fierce wind.
The sun got even paler.
"Don't people everywhere get broken hearts?" asked Orimar.
"Why should you stop shining on my kingdom just for that?"
"She stopped rising in the morning to greet me," said the sun.

"The Prince became King and he stayed indoors counting his money.
He didn't notice that his subjects stopped smiling and weren't happy.
They weren't happy because her muffins became ordinary.
Then she stopped baking and went to sleep and didn't wake up."
"You mean she died of a broken heart?" asked Orimar.
"She didn't die," said the sun, "she's still sleeping.

"She has dreams filled with clouds and rain and no one can wake her."
"But I never heard of her," said Orimar.
"Everyone forgot about her a long time ago," said the sun, "but not me.
I won't shine there again until she rises to greet me."
"Where is she sleeping?" asked Orimar.
"She is in a house all covered in vines, in the forest," replied the sun.

Just then a gust of wind thrust Orimar back into the clouds.
The motor for his wings started to make strange sounds.
His fuel ran out.
He went crashing down into the forest.
He was lucky that his wings got caught in the branch of a tree.
He had to detach himself and jump down from there.

Orimar looked around.
Somewhere in the forest the baker's daughter was sleeping.

He thought he could probably search for her the rest of his life.
But it turned out he had landed right at her doorstep.
He cut away the vines and entered.
Sure enough, a beautiful woman was lying on an ordinary bed.

Without hesitating Orimar kissed her on the lips.
Her eyes fluttered open and she looked into his.
Orimar looked so much like her prince that she thought he was.
"I knew it was all a dream," she said, "and that you would return.
We are all princes and princesses in the kingdom of love."
Orimar was overcome by her words and the music in her voice.

"My lady," he said, "I would never be parted from your good will.
If you would rise to greet the sun by my side, I would be honored."
She took his hand and rose from her bed.
She followed him all the way to the mountaintop.
When she looked up, the clouds suddenly disappeared.
The whole kingdom came outdoors for the first time in memory.

She went straight to the kitchen and started baking muffins.
The prince told the king that he would marry the baker's daughter.
The king said he had arranged a marriage with a lake princess.
Orimar told the king that he had to marry the baker's daughter.
If he didn't marry her the sun would stop shining.
Orimar offered the king a muffin and the king ate it.

The king smiled for the first time in his life.
He liked the way it felt and decided he wanted to keep smiling.
So he agreed to allow Orimar to marry the baker's daughter.
The young lovers lived together happily and one day became king and queen.
They still rise every morning to greet the sun and bake bread.
To this day Orimar's Kingdom is the Kingdom of Love.

FROM THE JOURNALS OF
SENATOR SIN

LETTER TO MY DAUGHTER

My only daughter, my substantial fortune will be yours one day, but what good will that be to you if you do not have sufficient knowledge to use it wisely and not be used? The most valuable gift I can bequeath to you is the sum of my experiences. So my dear this is the diary of the one and only Senator Sin. In the days and years to come I shall faithfully record my experiences and memories, for you. I hope that you, who look so much like I did at your age, shall find it useful.

I sometimes wonder how my mother might have spoken to me about her sexual experiences if she had ever dared. Would I have done anything differently? Would I have been better prepared for a world full of men? Her silence was a map with no boundaries drawn, and no indication of the names of landmarks like Treacherous Waters or The Land of Milk and Honey. My mother stopped off in The Valley of Dreams and still resides there, a place which I like to visit, but where I would never live.

Now that I am your mother and every day you race to embrace the beautiful and tender woman you will become, I find myself wanting fiercely to protect you from the crassness and even cruelty of men. I can only think of two ways to protect you. The first is to live forever and watch over you continually, not allowing a moment to pass when you are not directly within my loving gaze, never allowing any person unworthy of your grace to enter your exquisite consciousness. The other is to put before you both the beauty and the beast so that no matter what may happen to me, you will be able to distinguish between the two and decide for yourself which road to travel.

I did not become intimate with the desires of men until my tender breasts first budded. Until then I was convinced that the force of my thoughts and the expression in my eyes were my greatest powers. I played innocently with my own body, exploring every aspect of it, and was capable of giving myself pleasure. Having earned the respect of my schoolteachers, having spent hours reading, and hours again sketching with my art teacher, I was confident that the entire universe was there for me to explore. It never occurred to me that my changing appearance might influence the way in which my thoughts and talents would be regarded.

One morning before school (I attended an exclusive school in New York City, for the children of CEOs and movie stars), I shunned my jeans and baggy T-shirt, and put on a dress which my mother had bought for me a few weeks ago and which I had never worn before. I looked at myself in the mirror. The dress bounced off my rounding hips. It had a comfortably snug waistline, and darts which made the shape and swell of my breasts evident to the world. The word got around that day that I had stuffed my bra with socks. I found this out from Alvin, a boy in my class who I competed with for the best grades. "Everyone knows you stuffed your bra to fit your dress," he said. "How could everyone know that?" I asked. "Because Harriet said she saw you changing in the locker room and Harriet never lies," he said. "Well should I take my dress off so you can see my real breasts for yourself?" I asked. He ran away yelling to his buddies that I was going to take my dress off and they all surrounded me and started yelling, "Take it off, take it off." I thought about all the nude paintings I had studied in art books on the shelves in my home, and I figured that it would be a high-class thing to do. Anyway, when I was that age I could never resist a dare. I started to unzip my dress, which caused a great yell to go up among the boys surrounding me. The principal of the school came to see what the commotion was about. I got suspended for a week.

I considered the suspension a vacation from the tedious routine of school. I was already ahead on my homework and dove right into reading another Henry Miller novel. My attitude made my father angry, so he took all my novels away. My mother sent away the maid and made me sweep and mop and dust and iron every day. She said I had behaved like a low-class slut. "But what about all those paintings of nude women in those books on that shelf over there?" I asked. "That's different," my mother insisted, but she never explained why.

I still maintain a physical regimen that began when my brother and I worked out together, jogged together, stretched together, wrestled together. One afternoon that week, after I had cleaned the house to my mother's satisfaction, my father came upon my brother and I engaged in a fierce struggle, sweating in our sweat suits. I was laying across my brother and had him pinned to the ground. My father commanded me to get up instantly and go to my room. He spoke long into the night with my brother, and a few weeks later he was sent away to boarding school.

When I returned to school my competition with Alvin became more intense. It became more important to me to always come out on top in every subject. I was surprised when he took my hand during our advanced literature class, and held it. I yanked my hand from his and moved away. How could he get such an idea? I have a photographic memory. I never forget an insult. The teacher of that class was ugly. She made herself that way because she envied a beautiful woman like me who had an unforgettable face and figure and was also smarter than she was. English literature was my favorite subject. I spent hours deliberating over the exact way to express my thoughts in my essay assignments. Alvin and I both received As on our papers, but she often wrote little comments on the bottom of mine saying that if she discovered someone had helped me, or I had copied my essay from somewhere, my grade would be taken away. I should have paid more attention to her suspicions at the time, but I considered her jealousy of me contemptible and beneath the dignity of a response.

My mind was centered on someone else. My art teacher and I were spending many extracurricular hours sketching each other. When he drew me he spoke volumes about my lips, my eyes, and my long shapely legs. I was flattered. I watched him intently while he worked, and then I sketched him, admiring the muscles in his arms, his leather vest and long brown hair. I suggested that I would like to start sketching nudes. He said I was too young. I argued that I had studied nude sketches in hundreds of books, gone to the Met and the Guggenheim and plenty of other places, and now I wanted to do some nude sketching.

When I look back with the perspective I have now I think maybe even he wondered why he did it, an idiot taking orders from a mere child. My advanced literature teacher found me sitting in his lap with him sucking my breasts. At the time I thought it was really unfair that they fired him and expelled me.

My father blamed me. He told me I should get married and started looking around for a suitable husband. I protested that I was only fourteen. He said a woman like me needed to get married at a young age and settle into having kids. I protested that I wanted to get my doctorate. "I'll never get married!" I insisted.

I meant it when I said it but I didn't know it would turn out to be true. While I was yet a virgin I had already taken the first steps down my own path. I would be Senator Sin, a singularly beautiful, highly intelligent and sensual woman representing the feminine ideal for herself, and and not willing to give it up without a fight.

UN-NAMED FLOWER

I am a rare un-named flower. No one recognizes me when they gaze at me, because they have never heard of a flower like me, or stroked petals like mine before.

My scent is delicately intoxicating. Its essence is measured in precious drops of love, beads of sweat, streams of milk, rivers of emotions, sensations, libations.

Among all the common varieties I am misunderstood, misrepresented, often misguided, intimate with misfortune, but never feared or forgotten.

Women trust and love me, or envy and disparage me. Some look in my eye and read poetry there, others hate me because I am such a beautiful flower.

Men buy me, cut me, sell me, pluck me, poke their fingers around trying to find my center, put aspirin in my water and marvel at my resilience.

SMOKE

Go ahead and smoke.
Fill your lungs with it.
Send it out to the Atmosphere.
It's spiritual.
It's your connection to Heaven.
Communicate with the divine.
Share it.
Don't do it by yourself all the time.
Smoking is a social activity.
Smoking is good for your art.
No appetite?
Smoke and relax and eat.
That'll get your juices going.
Had a bad dream last night?
What was bad about it?
You woke up sweating?
Your heart was running a race of its own?
Smoke and forget all about it.
Smoke and you won't remember your dreams.
Smoke because you like it.
Smoke because you would rather sleep.
Smoke because you need to get in the mood.
Get in the mood for what?
In the mood for dancing?
In the mood for creating?
In the mood for love?
In the mood for a party?
In the mood to go to work?
In the mood to walk out in the cold?
In the mood to face the streets?
Smoke for courage.
Smoke and you'll get ideas.

Smoke and you'll get better ideas.
Smoke for writer's block.
Smoke for a bad stomach.
Smoke and relax.
Smoke and go to sleep.
Eat when you wake up.
Smoke and forget.
Forget you have gray hair.
Forget your keys.
Forget your dreams.
Forget when you woke up there was a strange man looking at you.
Forget your family hates you.
Forget your mother loves you.
Forget your address.
Forget you're an American.
Forget you're as guilty as everyone else.
Forget your phone number.
Forget where you put anything.
Forget there's a war on your block.
Forget you're a civilian.
Forget your father spit on you.
Forget you were gang-banged.
Forget you're perverted, twisted, and screwed.
Forget you lick your own wounds.
Forget about politics.
Forget what you're supposed to remember not to forget.
No one knows you're grieving.
Smoke and forget.
Smoke because it's cheap.
Cheaper than therapy.
Cheaper than Prozac.
Cheaper than a tropical vacation.

Keep your feelings to yourself.
Put them away on a dusty shelf.
Find the spirit in the air.
In the smoke.
Dirty politics got you down?
Don't understand the suffering in your hometown?
Want to leave but you're caught in quicksand?
Need the courage to take a stand?
Is that why you frown instead of smiling?
Smoke and go to sleep.
Smoke and do it in the morning.

A NIGHT IN THE LIFE

I am living with you, my daughter, in a new house. My mother is living there too. It is nice but I thought we were going to have it to ourselves. My mother shows me another place that she keeps. There is a noisy bedroom facing the street, and I think it is not as nice as the other place but I wouldn't mind taking this bedroom. I think that maybe after I put you to bed (you are quite young), at the other place, I could leave you there with my mother and I could come here to work and practice.

My mother shows me that there is an old washing machine in the bathroom. The paint is chipping on the walls, and water dripping from the faucet. She says that she might rent out the bathroom since no one is using it. She also shows me the kitchen. I realize that there is a woman up in a loft which I hadn't noticed. I climb the ladder and see that there is a big loft, and two women sitting up with their clothes on in bed. They are not friendly or unfriendly. They already live there.

I go to the kitchen and look outside. I see strangers lounging around. They seem dangerous and I want them to leave. I tell them to leave. They don't want to go. An elderly woman takes my right hand and inflicts pain on it, and won't let it go.

I decide I want to go to the swimming pool and get on a train to go there. I start to get dressed for it, but have problems getting my clothes on correctly. Finally I get on my overalls and then realize I put them on backwards. I decide to just leave them that way, since I'm just going to take them off again to go swimming. My father nods as I go by.

The swimming pool is crowded. I hang my white towel on the railing by the steps. It trails off into the water, most of it getting wet. I pull it back out again and then get in the pool. A big group of boys comes along wearing roller blades. They all get in the pool together and make it even more crowded. I try to get by them so I can swim, but have trouble. Finally, since they are all standing in two circles like they are having a meeting I ask them if they could move a little or have their meeting somewhere else. One of them grabs my breast and squeezes it. Other than that they ignore me. I yell at him that he shouldn't do that and I will have him arrested, but he obviously isn't worried about it. The other circle laughs at me and continues to make it hard for me to get by.

Finally I decide to just get out of the swimming pool. At the same time I see that they are all getting out too and putting their roller blades back on. So then I decide I want to go swimming with no bathing suit. My father says that that is against the rules and I can't do it. I get very angry and say I am going to go swimming and I do. Swimming naked feels good. I go back and forth under the water like a deep sea shark, feeling smooth and serene as the water passes along my skin. He gets angry and I get out of the pool. I see a sign clearly posted that says that nude swimming is against the rules. It makes me angry.

I get thrown into a prison cell in the city, with one other person. I figure out a way to escape through a hole in the window, but I struggle with the other person who doesn't want to let me get away. We struggle as I try to get out, but I decide to bide my time. The other person is on the ground. I climb up on a high loft, where the hole in the window is. I wait for the person to fall asleep and plan my escape. Finally I climb out and find myself at the top of a skyscraper.

Someone is climbing up the side of the building, pursuing me. I have a gun but can't load it.

Someone else is on the roof with me. I say this is pretty funny. Then I climb inside through a window. I am in a group with two other people I don't know, at a hospital, for more testing. I have tested positive for lymphatic cancer. The nurse offers us an aerosol can of deodorant to spray under our arms before she takes a swab. I get angry and tell her we don't need that cancer-causing stuff under our arms.

I run through the city streets with Erica Jong. She sees her dishes sitting out on a step. She grabs some, and I grab some for her. We run down an alley. A woman being chased by a man passes us by, running faster than we are. I'm thinking about trying to get to the apartment on 11th Street. We look around while we're standing up against the wall and see the guy who is running after the girl. When he sees us he starts chasing us instead. I throw a dish at him and start running again. I turn around to look, and see that he has almost caught up to me. I pose like I'm going to throw something else at him, but I really intend to kick him in the balls. I am frightened. When he gets close I kick my radiator and wake up.

TURNING THE SCREW

I wish your mother had taken you in her arms
put your mouth to her breast, whispered charms
and stroked you 'til you had your fill.

I wish your mother hadn't been beaten down
into the ground, wish she could have heard the sound
of love in your cries and seen it in your eyes.

I wish my father never spit on me,
I didn't have a long and twisted history,
we could have set each other free.

I wish your mother's mother didn't know mine,
they didn't stand on opposite sides of a line,
they could have linked arms instead of just dying.

I wish I didn't know where you were when you weren't with me,
what I know is true didn't have to be,
I knew how to be lonely.

I wish I could say I don't love you.
But you fuck me and I fuck you.
Isn't that what we're supposed to do?

The world was spinning before we came.
When we leave it will be the same.
We're just turning the screw.

VIRGIN MOTHER

I should explain.
I'm not asking for anything.

You can't give me a picket fence
to keep out nuclear waste,
sculptured faucets spouting
crystal clear water,
a roof to deflect missiles and acid rain
from falling on us as we consummate our vows.
No, I'm not asking for security
not asking you to say you
thought of me yesterday
won't love my sister tomorrow
will take care of me when I get cancer
won't infect me with a lethal disease
that our children won't be mutants
or that I won't cry alone.

I should explain.
I'm not looking for a father

for my daughter,
don't need authority,
morality for me,
a pill to set me free,
forearms or omnipotence.
I wear an untarnished
scarlet letter
I'll give to my daughter
like a family treasure.

I should explain.
I'm a virgin mother.

I'm always looking for my son,
my lover,
meeting him with groping eyes in bedrooms,
embracing him by riverbanks,
libating him among gravestones,
stroking the life in our bones.
There's no need to tell me lies.

I should explain.
I'm not asking for anything.

Just bring me a little food
for me to prepare
a rhythm we can dance to
and offer as a prayer.
Just bring your body
and soul.

WEATHER COCK

Which way
will the wind whip
my weather cock today?
If it blows North
where will I be?
Will it ever point at me?
Will it ever stay?

A DAY IN THE LIFE

(Back When You and I Lived off Welfare Payments)

"Write it all down," she said,
as I got out of the car on the corner.

"Yeah you're right I'll do that."

Thinking:

'I'm lucky to be sweating the rent
lucky to be alive
lucky I escaped being mugged yesterday,
lucky to be walking talking breathing moving
outwardly healthy
or near healthy
or something.'

I went upstairs, turned the key and entered, always feeling peculiar without you there, without hearing your slow steady breath in slumber, even though I know you are in good hands, going to bed without washing my face, dropping my clothes on the floor by the bed, among a pile of clothes, all mine, some clean some dirty, all hand-me-downs, practically all donated to me by my mother. Falling into a stupor sleep thinking I need to change the sheets and bring the laundry out.

The phone rang at seven in the morning.
It was Lover Man,
who I told my girlfriend driving the car
I had no feelings about anymore.
He was on the corner.
I had no idea if he had been out all night,

or visiting his latest fancy

after leaving me at the party.
I didn't ask.
I didn't care.

I was naked and didn't bother to cover myself.
I opened the door still groggy grumbled something,
went back to bed and rolled a joint.
He stripped and started rubbing me.

"I'm ovulating,"
I told him.

"OK."

Sucking on the edges of my velvety petals, with two weeks'
growth of downy fur, the amount of time which had passed since
the last time he had come to my bed.

"You know I'm sex starved don't you."

"Quit complaining."

I made no sound
but felt liquid fire spreading from my center outward
relaxed into the feeling
preferring to remain on the edge of sleep.
His stem was drooping.
I started rubbing it up and down.
We kissed.

I didn't need to have feelings for water to flow,
to join his stem to my center
and hold it there.

He groaned.

I cling to him for the only thing he offers me.
Softening to respond to his tremors
with wet whirls of confused emotion.
Humming softly in my throat
he suddenly disconnects from me
and is gone.
Me wishing he could have held on a little longer.

Thankful at least that he has that much control.

I rolled over and went back to sleep.
Thinking of another man who left me unsatisfied.
Wishing he was in my bed tonight.

I think longing could kill me after awhile
like a heart attack.

I got scared of my new laptop.
I left it sitting in the closet for a few days
because I couldn't get it to do what I wanted it to do.
But this afternoon I took it out again.
When I called customer service I didn't understand their answer.
I haven't even started hooking up the modem,
bought a split line for my telephone,
or any of that stuff.

But then I did get strep throat
and was laying up with a 102 fever for three days,
and then you got it but not half as bad as me,
and now you're driving me up the wall,
and I'm probably driving you up the wall too.
My first theater production was more appreciated
than I thought it would be, or should be,
even though I couldn't even be there.

I have this vague notion
that I'll get to the print shop today
and the copy machine won't be working
for some reason that no one will understand.
I'm not sure I have enough money
to make copies anyway.

My favorite author called me today,
and thanked me for thanking her,
and when she said she liked it,
I stopped and thought about that for a moment.
But there is no time to stop.
There is so much to do,
and so much I am leaving undone.

Perhaps I really am a fool.

Visit the Cinasphere at:
www.cinader.com

Recordings by Martha Cinader available at:
www.cinader.com/po'azzyo'azz/recordings/links.html
including the new cd "Living It."

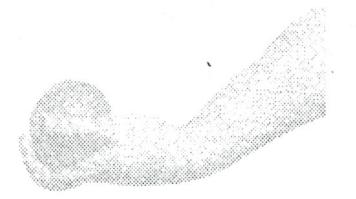